# AYR
## PAST & PRESENT

### DANE LOVE

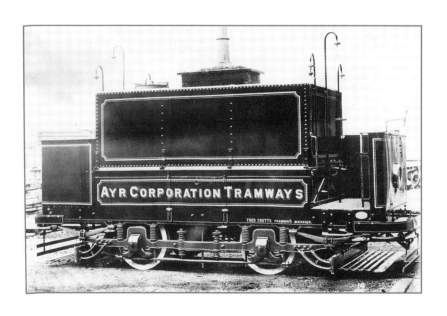

SUTTON PUBLISHING

Sutton Publishing Limited
Phoenix Mill · Thrupp · Stroud
Gloucestershire · GL5 2BU

First published 2003

Copyright © Dane Love, 2003

Title page photograph: Ayr Corporation
Tramways, car number 17, which operated
variously as a water car, snow plough and
rail grinder. (*Author's Collection*)

**British Library Cataloguing in Publication Data**
A catalogue record for this book is available from the
British Library.

ISBN 0-7509-3257-0

Typeset in 10.5/13.5 Photina.
Typesetting and origination by
Sutton Publishing Limited.
Printed and bound in England by
J.H. Haynes & Co. Ltd, Sparkford.

The Twa Brigs, *c.* 1900. (Frank McKee)

# CONTENTS

Introduction                                    5

1.  Streets & Shops                            9

2.  Ayr at Work                                41

3.  Health, Rest & Recreation                  61

4.  Honest Men & Bonie Lasses                  79

5.  There was a Lad                            93

6.  Around & About                            109

    Acknowledgements                          128

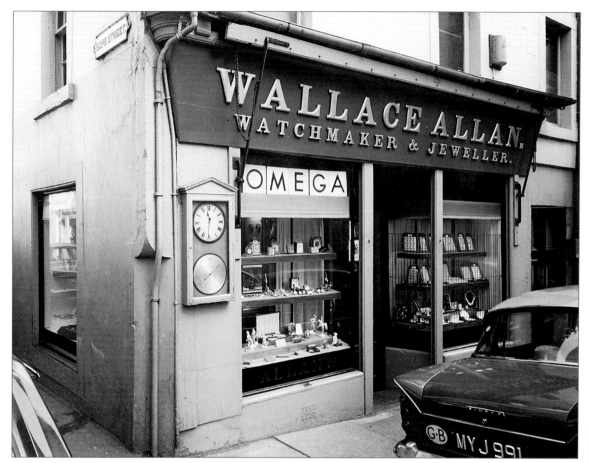

Wallace Allan's jewellery shop, *c.* 1965. (*Grant Allan*)

# INTRODUCTION

The Royal Burgh of Ayr has existed since 21 May 1205, when King William the Lion granted the town a charter. About ten years earlier the king established his 'New Castle of Ayr' at the mouth of the River Ayr, and used it to help establish law and order in the surrounding sheriffdom of Ayr. From that day onward Ayr has been the county town and main centre of administration for a wide area of the west of Scotland.

There was probably some form of settlement at the mouth of the River Ayr before the arrival of the New Castle. Mesolithic finds have been discovered in the locality, and a few prehistoric relics survive, probably relics from the Stone Age, such as the standing stone at the end of Stonefield Avenue in Doonfoot. The Romans are thought to have built a road from Galloway through what is now Dalmellington and down the valley of the River Doon to Ayr. It is claimed that Mill Street occupies the line of this route, which may have headed to an earlier fortification or harbour.

The mists of antiquity cloud the early history of the town. Early references in the exploits of the Vikings, William Wallace and Robert the Bruce may have been elaborated over the centuries. Wallace had many associations with the town, and it was here English forces imprisoned him for a time. No doubt he burned the town's barns in May 1297, but whether he killed hundreds of enemy English within, or none, is still debated. The castle had been taken by the English in 1306; Bruce recaptured it in 1314.

Ayr had a couple of important early ecclesiastical buildings, all trace of which have gone. The first Dominican friary in Scotland was established here in 1230, and the site of the Blackfriars' monastery was approximately where the Auld Kirk hall is now. Almost next door, where the present Auld Kirk stands, was the Greyfriars' monastery, occupied by Franciscan friars and established in 1474. Other early sites include St Leonard's hospital (which operated in the fifteenth century), Dalmilling chapel, and the refuge for lepers, founded by Bruce.

During the time of the Commonwealth Cromwell ordered the construction of a citadel between the town and the sea, of which fragments of the walls survive. The citadel was beneficial to Ayr in more ways than one, principally in sheltering the town from the sea, preventing blowing sands from engulfing the Sandgate, as had happened for centuries before.

The town grew slowly from its High Street and Sandgate beginnings. Being the administrative centre of the county gave it some degree of importance. Many of the

Aerial view of the southern end of Ayr, *c.* 1950. (*Liz Kelly*)

county families erected their own town houses in the burgh, two important ones – Loudoun Hall and Lady Cathcart's House – surviving. In the early nineteenth century these older buildings were abandoned in favour of more spacious and salubrious Georgian houses, erected around the southern side of the town.

A market town, attracting farmers from all over the county, Ayr was also an important seaport, which traded in a variety of goods, notably cloth, wine, tobacco, coal and citrus fruit, and was Scotland's most important west coast port for a time. There were a few coalmines on the north side of the river, and the arrival of the railway in 1840 extended the possibilities for trade. Over the years the town has had various iron foundries, sawmills, shipyards, chemical manufacturers, carpet works, woollen mills and starch works. Today there is little heavy industry, most of the employment being in the service industries.

The eighteenth and nineteenth century saw Ayr growing in importance, and the harbour was repaired and extended accordingly. This new wealth was shown off through the creation of fine terraces and the establishment of a national bank. Known as Douglas, Heron & Co., this was founded in 1769 but was to crash spectacularly three years later. New developments in the town were growing apace, including the formation of industries, gasworks, new communities at Wallacetown in

1760 and Content shortly afterwards, and the erection of some fine municipal buildings, including the Town Hall and Court House.

Major developments came in the early twentieth century following the launch of a municipal electricity supply in 1896 and the establishment of a tram service in 1901, which ran until 1931. The railway company acquired the harbour in 1919, and various improvements followed.

Tourism has played an important part in the life of the town over the years. Situated at the head of a sandy beach, with fine views to the mountains of Arran, Ayr has been a popular destination for holidaymakers. When tourism first became popular Ayr was quick to see its potential, and welcomed visitors by steamer, being an important halt for those cruising 'doon the watter' from Glasgow. Numerous hotels and boarding houses were opened in the town, in particular in the First Ward part of the town, where many of the large private houses were converted. At the former naval training camp near to the Heads of Ayr, Billy Butlin established a popular holiday camp, which attracted visitors from far and wide.

One person has done more for the tourism industry than any other in Ayr – Robert Burns. The so-called national bard was born at nearby Alloway (now part of the town) in 1759 and went on to become one of the most internationally

Burns Statue Square, *c.* 1950. (*Frank McKee*)

Ayrshire Philharmonic Operatic Society's production of *Utopia Ltd.* 1956. (*Ann Watson*)

recognised poets of all time. His birthplace has been preserved, and a variety of locations associated with him throughout the parish survive.

Today Ayr is an important commercial centre for a wide hinterland. The main shopping streets in the centre of the town have been augmented over the years by new indoor shopping centres, as well as large out-of-town supermarkets and retail parks.

The population of Ayr has grown almost consistently since its foundation. In 1801 there were 5,492 people living in the town. This increased to 7,606 in 1831; 9,308 in 1861; 11,149 in 1891; 33,000 in 1911; 36,783 in 1931; 43,000 in 1961; 48,000 in 1991; and over 50,000 today.

# 1

# *Streets & Shops*

Sandgate, *c.* 1905. Looking north up the Sandgate, or
Sandgate Street as it is named on the postcard. Standing
in the middle of the road like this is inadvisable today!
(*Author's Collection*)

Sandgate, *c.* 1945. The Sandgate is probably Ayr's oldest street, stretching from the site of the Malt Cross southwards to the Sandgate Port. This postcard depicts the street looking south, with the Town Hall on the left, complete with police office, at the junction with High Street. The buildings on the right have hardly altered, only the shop premises changing hands with seemingly ever-increasing rapidity. Although most folk think of them as part of the Sandgate, the buildings on the right are actually part of New Bridge Street. (*Author's Collection*)

Sandgate, 2003. The Town Hall has changed little and the streetscape is much the same, only Poundstretcher having a more modern facia. Now much busier with one way traffic, most of the buildings on the right are occupied by bars or cafés. The police station has long since gone, though note the police van in the correct position! On the ground the cross and surrounding cobbles mark the site of the Malt Cross, rebuilt in 1697 but removed in 1778 when New Bridge Street was created. (*Dane Love*)

Sandgate, *c.* 1950. This view of the Sandgate looks north towards the magnificent 217-feet steeple of the Town Hall and across the New Bridge towards the Carnegie Library. The buildings on the right, seen from the junction with Newmarket Street north towards the Town Hall, were at one time some of Ayr's busiest shops. Stephen & Pollock, booksellers and publishers, occupied the premises on the immediate right, at the junction with Newmarket Street, for many years. Hugh Pollock (1888–1971) was the first husband of the famous writer Enid Blyton. (*James McCarroll*)

Sandgate, 2003. The old building on the left of the upper photograph has been replaced by the modern Royal Bank of Scotland building, dating from 1973. The former bank next door is currently empty, and just visible beyond is the restored Lady Cathcart's House, which probably dates from the sixteenth century. Shops still occupy the east side of the street, among them jewellers, hairdressers, a boutique, an off-licence, gift shop and Chinese restaurant. (*Dane Love*)

Lady Cathcart's House, *c.* 1980. The building at the corner of Sandgate and Cathcart Street was a much-altered structure shorn of its original appearance. Adjoining the Bank of Scotland (by Alexander Petrie in 1877), the building had been occupied by a variety of shops over the years, the upper floors serving as flats. In the mid-1980s there were proposals to demolish it, but on discovering that the ground floor was vaulted campaigns to save it commenced. In 1989 it was acquired by the Scottish Historic Buildings Trust. (*Fred Westcott*)

Lady Cathcart's House, 2003. Restoration work commenced in 1991 under the guidance of architects Simpson & Brown. It was discovered that part of the building dated from around 1600 and incorporated an arcaded ground floor, similar to older commercial premises found in some Scots burghs. This could not be rebuilt, but the traditional corbie-stepped gables and dormer windows were restored. The local Tourist Information Centre now occupies the lower floor. Tradition claims that this building was the birthplace of John Loudon MacAdam (1756–1836), the celebrated road maker. (*Dane Love*)

Wellington Square, *c.* 1930. This square was laid out in 1806 as one of the new developments in the town. At the west end, seen here, is the classical frontage of the Sheriff Court, erected in 1818–22 to plans by Robert Wallace. To the left is the Pavilion Theatre. In the centre of the square is the cenotaph of 1924, originally with 817 names inscribed on it. On the left of the picture is the statue of James Neill (1810–57), to the right is Sir James Fergusson (1832–1907), and framed by the portico of the courthouse is the 13th Earl of Eglinton (1812–61). (*Author's Collection*)

Wellington Square, 2003. Little has changed in the overall appearance of the square. The central area is more enclosed than it once was, now surrounded by hedges and gardens. The statues and cenotaph have been joined by a memorial to John Loudon MacAdam, unveiled by the Institution of Municipal and County Engineers in 1936, and the obelisk to former Provost, Primrose Kennedy (1800–63), originally located in Fort Street, but moved here in 1993. (*Dane Love*)

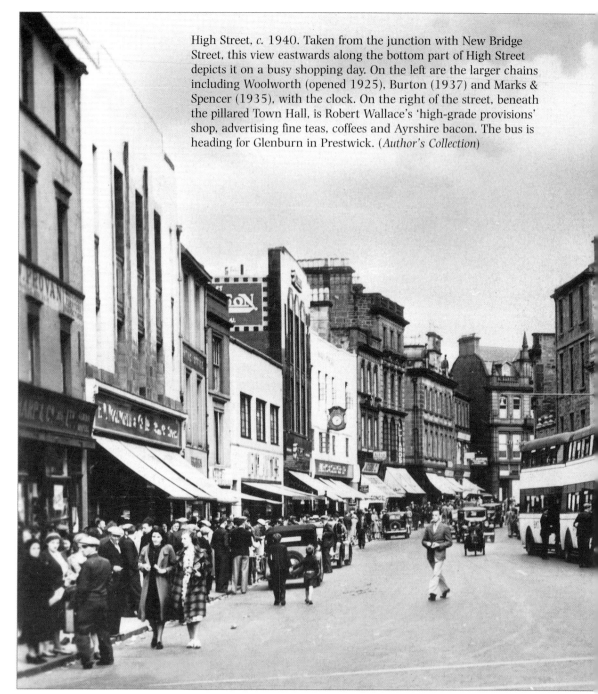

High Street, *c.* 1940. Taken from the junction with New Bridge Street, this view eastwards along the bottom part of High Street depicts it on a busy shopping day. On the left are the larger chains including Woolworth (opened 1925), Burton (1937) and Marks & Spencer (1935), with the clock. On the right of the street, beneath the pillared Town Hall, is Robert Wallace's 'high-grade provisions' shop, advertising fine teas, coffees and Ayrshire bacon. The bus is heading for Glenburn in Prestwick. (*Author's Collection*)

*Inset:* High Street, 2003. The streetscape has hardly changed over the last seventy years. The roadway has been partially pedestrianised – only buses, taxis and disabled drivers are allowed along it today. Still busy with shoppers, only Woolworth's is still in the same premises, though its upper façade has changed. While Burton's has moved premises its mural sign survives, but is gradually fading. The only real change is the erection of the brick-built Marks & Spencer premises of 1974, at the far corner, and the more congruous shops to its left. (*Dane Love*)

High Street, *c.* 1910. The dogleg in the High Street is known as the Fish Cross. This was at one time the centre of town, where traffic crossing the Auld Brig entered the High Street. The Fish Cross was where fish was sold from 1547 until 1853, when the harbour fish market was opened. The first building on the right was the Star Inn. A pend through the building led to the Corn Exchange. The fine building next door (with the sun shades) was erected in the 1880s to plans of John Mercer. (*Author's Collection*)

High Street, 2003. A new statue of a man holding a fish has been erected on the site of the original Fish Cross, the work of Malcolm Robertson in 1995. At first glance the buildings look similar, but the inn has been demolished, replaced by a brick-built shop with a modern pend. BHS next door occupies a modern building erected in 1984, incorporating the original façades of its predecessors. The Buttermarket was relocated here in 1869, from Newmarket Street. (*Dane Love*)

Wallace Allan, *c. 1925.* Wallace Allan established his jewellery and watchmaking business around 1873, originally in the building next door to the present shop, where he moved at the end of the nineteenth century. Wallace Allan was a local councillor for a time – he is pictured standing with his son Robert. In about 1920 he made a copy of the Eiffel Tower that doubled as a time-check, a ball falling at the precise second. This was controlled by a signal sent from the Paris Observatory. (*Grant Allan*)

Wallace Allan, 2003. The present Wallace Allan shop is an attractively restored building of the eighteenth century or earlier. At one time it was the Wallace Tavern, so-called because Sir William Wallace was held in the tolbooth here for a time. Today Wallace and Grant Allan, grandson and great-grandson of the founder, run the business. (*Dane Love*)

The Isle, *c.* 1910. This part of the High Street, where the narrow Hope Street, or 'Back o' the Isle' passes behind the Clydesdale Bank building, shown in the centre, was the original site of the Laigh Tolbooth and Meal Market. A statue of Sir William Wallace on the building shown between the tram and the car commemorates the spot where he was held in Ayr and was taken for dead. The bank building is known as Winton Buildings and was erected in 1844, the Clydesdale Bank moving there in 1856. Note the Crown Inn on the left. (*James McCarroll*)

The Isle, 2003. The Winton Buildings have been painted and were occupied by the Clydesdale Bank until 2002. In front of them is a sculpture depicting 'The Poet and the World', the work of Doug Cocker, unveiled in 1996 to mark the bicentenary of Robert Burns' death. Most of the buildings on the left remain unchanged, apart from the smaller shop. As the area is partially pedestrianised, there is now more room for wider pavements and the planting of trees, which soften the lines. (*Dane Love*)

High Street, 1933. Taken from an upper window in the Winton Buildings, this postcard depicts the High Street looking south towards the Wallace Tower. The Imperial Bar was one of twenty-six inns in the High Street at that time. Next door is the classical Union Bank, dating from 1856. Hepworths and Boots the Chemist follow. The tramlines are still visible, but the service was replaced by buses in 1931, the poles for the cables having been converted into lamp standards. The single-storey bus is heading for Prestwick Toll. (*Author's Collection*)

High Street, 2003. Without the benefit of first-floor access, the viewpoint is lower in this photograph. The inn has closed and is currently occupied by a boutique. The ground floor of the bank was refaced with Creetown granite in 1963. It latterly became a branch of the Halifax, but this was closed in 2003. The streetscape on the right is similar as far as the magnificent 1902 Georgian Bank of Scotland building, after which modern shops of 1968 and 1973 are occupied by Littlewoods and other chains. (*Dane Love*)

Gaumont Cinema, *c.* 1965. The Gaumont was one of six cinemas that existed in Ayr at one time. These included Green's Playhouse, the Ritz, the Orient (opened 1932), the Regal (opened 1936) and the Odeon (opened 1938). Previously the Gaumont was known as the Picture House. Of the six cinemas, only the Odeon survives, located in Burns Statue Square. Green's was converted into a bingo hall, the Orient is now Babylon nightclub, the Ritz is a snooker club and the Regal became a motor showroom. (*Fred Westcott*)

High Street, 2003. The Gaumont was demolished to make way for the Littlewoods store, erected in 1968. In a small garden behind the Gaumont was a statue of the Revd John Welch (1568–1622), one of the first ministers to suffer for his adherence to Presbyterianism. When the shop was built the statue was removed to the Auld Kirk, and all that remains to mark the site is a plaque on the wall. In 2002 Littlewoods was rebuilt internally to create more shops on the High Street, including Ottakar's bookshop, Iceland food sales and JJB sports shop. (*Dane Love*)

Wallace Tower, *c.* 1905. This edifice was erected in 1833 to plans of Thomas Hamilton. There is no connection with William Wallace other than the present building incorporates a statue of the great freedom fighter. Nearby stood the Barns of Ayr that he is traditionally said to have set alight, killing hundreds of English soldiers. To the left can be seen the Ayr Arms Hotel, run by Mathew Dickie. On the opposite side of the street is the Ailsa Bar. (*Author's Collection*)

Wallace Tower, 2003. The tower has had some restoration work done to it over the years and today remains a prominent landmark in the town. Most of the shop premises remain quite unchanged at first glance, but those to the left are in the main only retained façades, the remainder of the buildings, with their narrow fronts, being removed and replaced by the large Kyle Shopping Centre, erected in 1987. On the right the redevelopment has been piecemeal, rather than comprehensive. (*Dane Love*)

High Street, 1987. A number of old shops in the High Street were demolished as part of the new Kyle Centre development. This photograph shows work under way in the late winter of 1987, the High Street buildings coming down while the new shopping centre was going up behind. One of the demolished buildings (no. 181) was traditionally claimed to be where William Wallace escaped from pursuing Englishmen by jumping from the first floor. This was thereafter known as Wallace's Window, and a raised cobble in the street marked where he had landed. (*Fred Westcott*)

High Street, 2003. The new premises erected in the High Street were designed in a traditional manner, so that they fit in with the rest of the street. What used to be Murray Brothers' woollen mill in the upper photograph are the premises 'To Let' in the lower picture. Few would associate the buildings with the end of the twentieth century, but the Virgin Megastore and $O_2$ building is dated 1987. (*Dane Love*)

High Street, 1987. The façades of 209–13 High Street were retained in the new Kyle Centre, and a new roof was added above, copying the traditional style. The architects of the modern works were Shepherd Robson with Cowie, Torry & Partners, whereas the façade above the present Au Naturale was the work of James McDerment in 1862, and that next door to the left was designed by Murdoch & Lockhart in 1909. (*Fred Westcott*)

High Street, 2003. The Kyle Centre was the first large indoor shopping centre to be erected in Ayr. It opened in 1988 and contained a number of shops all under one roof. Linking the High Street with Carrick Street, the centre also boasts the Lighthouse café at first-floor level, and a wishing-well water feature in the centre, with monies raised dedicated to local charities. (*Dane Love*)

High Street and Wallace Tower, *c.* 1913. Taken from the junction of High Street with Alloway and Kyle streets, this postcard shows the top of the street looking back down towards the Wallace Tower. The Windsor Restaurant on the right was long established, and to the right of it was a bakery. On the left-hand side of the street were the Plough and Sun inns, catering for thirsty travellers. The Plough Inn, which was erected in 1904 to plans of J. & H.V. Eaglesham, still has its name carved in the sandstone façade. (*James McCarroll*)

*Inset:* High Street and Wallace Tower, 2003. Most of the buildings remain unchanged in this view from the top end of the High Street. The roadway is now restricted to certain vehicles, such as buses, taxis, disabled drivers and delivery vans. The traditional inns have gone, to be replaced by Café Biba, a licensed restaurant, and financial premises, such as Abbey National and Woolwich banks. The Cancer Research shop is just one of many charity shops to have appeared over the years. (*Dane Love*)

Alloway Street, 1927. Alloway Street links the top of the High Street with Burns Statue Square. This postcard view is taken looking from the Square. On the left is the Ayrshire & Galloway Hotel, followed by Anderson Brothers' Union House (which sold all kinds of clothing) after Dalblair Road junction. The three-storey building to the left of the tram is Hourston's department store, opened in 1896. To the right is the Palais de Danse, occupying the former Royal Scots Fusiliers' Drill Hall (with flag pole, erected in 1901), and next door is the Athole Arms Inn of 1900. (*James McCarroll*)

Alloway Street, 2003. The Ayrshire & Galloway Hotel survives, but most of the other premises are now occupied by other businesses. The houses of Killoch Place next to the hotel have been replaced by modern shops, and Union House is now a bathroom showroom. What was the Palais de Danse became the Bobby Jones ballroom, reinventing itself over the years as a disco and nightclub as fashions in music changed. The inn is still a public house, known as Findlay's. (*Dane Love*)

Burns Statue Square, 1907. Two statues adorn the Square, that to the national bard (to the left), and a second one commemorating the Royal Scots Fusiliers who were killed in the Boer War. Left of the statue are the large houses of Killoch Place, some of which were joined together to create the Beresford Temperance Hotel. To the right are premises occupied by Morrison's Restaurant, a billiards room and T. Kerr's bakery. Above it was the Burns Statue Hotel. (*Author's Collection*)

Burns Statue Square, 2003. The buildings on the right remain unchanged, other than new occupants in the shops. The Temperance Hotel has been replaced by modern shops. At the southern end of Killoch Place (the far left on the picture) is a modern building now occupied by CKD Galbraith, but built as a bank on the site of a branch of the British Linen Bank. The Fusiliers' statue has been moved a few times, and Burns' statue is rather lost among the trees when viewed from this angle. (*Dane Love*)

Burns Statue Square, c. 1910. Taken looking in the opposite direction, this postcard depicts the northern side of the Square, with the large Station Hotel at the east end. On the right is the curved wall surrounding Beresford Park, at one time the home ground of Ayr Football Club, which played here in the 1880s before moving to Somerset Park in 1888, home now of Ayr United. The park was also used for the local cattle show. (*Author's Collection*)

Burns Statue Square, 2003. The statues are still here and the buildings along the side of the street remain virtually unchanged, but this part of the street has been closed off to through traffic and landscaped. The site of the football ground has been built upon, now occupied by a tall office block (known as Burns' House), the Odeon cinema and Blockbuster video hire. (*Dane Love*)

Station Hotel, *c.* 1905. Andrew Galloway, chief engineer with Glasgow and South Western Railway, was the designer of the Station Hotel, erected in 1886. Previously a smaller station building (Townhead station) occupied the site, opened on 7 August 1856. The new station incorporated a large hotel, built at a cost of £50,000, and the burgh surveyor, John Mercer, wrote that 'I was very much pleased with [the plans] and have been sounding their praises so much that the Provost, Magistrates &c are quite on the qui vive to see them.' (*Author's Collection*)

Station Hotel, 2003. The Fusiliers' statue has been relocated owing to to road realignments, but still faces across the busy street towards the Station Hotel. Today the hotel has seventy-four bedrooms, the Kyle Restaurant, Locker Room Bar and Gallery Lounge. No longer owned by the railway company, it is part of the Edinburgh Inns group. Victorian visitors would be amazed at the en-suite toilets, satellite televisions and telephones in every room! Mind you, they would also gasp at today's prices! What was Simson and McCulloch's shops in the older picture is at present occupied by O'Briens, an Irish-themed bar. (*Dane Love*)

River Street, 1975. Viewed from the southern end of the Auld Brig, River Street links the Auld and New bridges. At the right is the Black Bull Inn, one of the oldest inns still functioning in the town. Robert Burns' father came here to interview John Murdoch as a possible teacher for Robert. Next door was part of the extended inn, originally with stables behind, but in later years offering 'cabs, carriages and motor cars' for hire. The building with the gablets was the River Street Mission Hall, erected in 1878 as a hall for the Darlington church. (*Fred Westcott*)

River Street, 2003. Most of the buildings look much as they did in the top photograph, although one or two buildings have been demolished and new ones erected on the same site, in particular that to the left of the former mission hall. The tall chimney has gone, and stretching behind the frontage to River Street is the modern Asda store, with its multi-storey car park. (*Dane Love*)

New Bridge Street, *c.* 1960. Taken from what was known as Darlington Road, this view is of South Harbour and New Bridge streets. The bow-fronted building on the far side of the bridge dates from 1787 and was erected by Alexander Stevens, builder of the first New Bridge, for himself. At the time of this postcard it was occupied by John Thomson, chemist. Next door was West Coast Fisheries followed by the Ayr Café. On South Harbour Street were a furniture store, Gibson's Anchor Tavern and a branch of the Kilmarnock Co-op, opened in 1896. (*Author's Collection*)

New Bridge Street, 2003. The view has hardly changed, only the redeveloped shops to the left of Stevens' building being much different. Note, however, the lost gablet and dormers on the third building in New Bridge Street. Next to Stevens' building can be seen the arched pend that formerly led to the stable yard associated with the King's Arms Hotel, one of Ayr's principal coaching inns, located on the High Street. South Harbour Street now has an empty shop at the corner, the Anchor Bar has changed its façade and the Co-op premises are now a bookmaker's shop. (*Dane Love*)

South Harbour Street, *c.* 1900. Taken from South Harbour Street and looking into the entrance of the Boat Vennel, this early postcard depicts what even in 1900 was described as 'a bit of auld Ayr'. The tall steeple of the Town Hall is the only instantly recognisable feature today, unless one can peel away some of the buildings to reveal the Loudoun Hall, at that time surrounded by smaller premises, including the Union Tavern. The Loudoun Hall was erected in about 1513, making it the oldest surviving building in the town. (*Author's Collection*)

Loudoun Hall, 2003. The antiquity of Loudoun Hall was recognised in the early twentieth century when the Marquis of Bute saved the building from demolition. Between 1946 and 1948 restoration of what was now a slum tenement began. The surrounding buildings were partially cleared away, leaving a garden area occupying what used to be the Union Tavern. At the entrance to the Boat Vennel is a bronze model of the building. Local groups use the hall as a meeting place, which is open to the public on occasions. The lower floor is vaulted, and in an upper room a stone aumbry can be seen. (*Dane Love*)

Wallace Street, *c.* 1985. This photograph was taken prior to the demolition of the west side of Wallace Street in preparation for the erection of the present Asda store. At the time of construction it was intended that the shop was going to be a Fine Fare store, but by the time it opened Fine Fare had been taken over and the shop became Gateway and later Asda. (*Fred Westcott*)

George Street, 2003. The same perspective is not possible as the line of Wallace Street was built over, and we can only look down the bottom stump of George Street. The Asda store is on the right, and blocks of flats occupy the corner with John Street. On the left are some traditional buildings that survive in George Street, erected in 1851–3, though when built were originally known as Gordon Place. (*Dane Love*)

River Street, *c.* 1900. Taken from what was Gordon Place (renamed as part of George Street), this view shows the north end of the Auld Brig, looking back to the rear of the High Street shops. The building on the left was Speir's planeworks, which operated from around 1840. The small shops next door included a couple of tobacconists and Hunter's Stores, built on the site of the ancient Bridge Port, one of the early gates defending the town. (*James McCarroll*)

River Street, 2003. The former planeworks is now a restaurant, having been a tearoom and café for a number of years. The little shop premises have gone, leaving only a few ruined walls behind iron railings, often mistaken for the remains of the Bridge Port. (*Dane Love*)

Main Street, *c.* 1967. This view of the bottom end of Main Street was taken from the Newton Cross, looking towards what was the Orient Picture House, erected in 1932 to plans by Albert Gardner. The white building on the left was originally the Forester's Arms, but it later became Graham's Bar. The inn may have been founded in 1836. Next door was a tyre-fitting garage. At one time cars were driven into the yard and on to a turntable that allowed them to be turned around ready to exit back on to the Main Street. (*Fred Westcott*)

Main Street, 2003. Most of the shops between the inn and the Orient (now Babylon nightclub) were demolished to make way for the MFI furniture showroom. The inn on the left is now The Brig, and the little shop is now The Wee Curiosity Shop. (*Dane Love*)

Picken's butcher's shop. *c.* 1930. The firm of Picken Brothers has been in existence since 1870. This photograph depicts the staff standing outside their premises at 71 Main Street, Newton-upon-Ayr. The business operated both a butchers and bakers, seen here in two adjoining premises. The male baker was William Dickie. The butchers on the right were David Picken (left) and Alex Picken (right). The butcher boy in the centre is unknown. (*Gordon Picken*)

Picken's butcher's shop, 2003. Still operating after 133 years, the business still offers both bakery items and butcher meat from the same premises, though the business is now known as A. Picken & Sons. Today the business is run by the brothers Gordon and Colin Picken. There is a second shop located at 27 Alloway Street in Ayr and a third in Maybole High Street. (*Dane Love*)

The Royal Café, *c.* 1932. Located in Newton's Main Street, the Royal Café was opened in 1925 by Antonio Mancini, who arrived in London from Italy at the end of the nineteenth century, and moved to Glasgow then Ayr in 1910. By 1913 Antonio opened his first ice cream shop at his house in King Street. In 1940 Michele Mancini (1917–1993, seen in the photograph) took over, before retiring in 1991. In 1935 a first-floor flat was added to the café. Between the 1930s and 1950s the firm supplied many local outlets, especially seafront businesses. (*Philip Mancini*)

The Royal Café, 2000. A lorry ran into the front of the café in 1999, destroying part of the building. A new façade was created in 2000, when this photograph of Michele and Philip Mancini was taken. The business still supplies up to 200 flavours of ice cream on a wholesale basis, as well as running a traditional Italian style café, selling fish and chips, and ices to take away. Philip Mancini was President of the Ice Cream Alliance in 1993–4. He was placed first in the National Ice Cream Competition 2001 for dairy ice cream. (*Philip Mancini*)

Prestwick Road, *c.* 1925. The long road north from the New Bridge towards Prestwick has gradually been built up over the years, and the smaller communities of Newton-upon-Ayr and New Prestwick incorporated into an ever-expanding town. This postcard depicts Prestwick Road as seen looking north from Tam's Brig. On the left is the tower of North Newton Parish Church. This was erected in 1885 to plans of John Murdoch. In front of it is D. Allan & Sons' coal merchants. Next to the small confectionery shop on the right is the start of McCall's Avenue. (*James McCarroll*)

Prestwick Road, 2003. The church was renamed St James's in 1904, but it still stands virtually unchanged, only its little roof on the tower having been removed. The former confectionery shop has now become the Mediterranean pizza, kebab, curry and burger take-away, tastes that the passing trade eighty years ago would not have experienced. This part of the street is known as Tam's Brig, the road crossing the main railway line hereabouts. 'Tam' may have been Thomas MacCreath, farmer at Bellesleyhill, who wanted to be first to cross the new railway bridge in 1852. (*Dane Love*)

Macrorie's grocery, 1953. There are numerous smaller shop premises beyond the main shopping streets of the town. Mrs S. Macrorie's grocery was located at 52 Mill Street, and is shown here decorated for the coronation of Queen Elizabeth in 1953. On sale within are a number of goods still extant today, including Brasso, Brooke Bond Tea and Scott's porridge oats, and some no longer available, such as Rinso, KY table vinegar and Oxydol. Previously Mrs Marion Walker occupied the shop, and before that it was the premises of Hugh MacKinnon, ham curer. At that time it was numbered 50½! (*Isobel McGarvey*)

Asda, 2003. Shopping in Ayr has changed considerably over the past fifty years. Most of the small groceries have gone, the residents shopping instead at large superstores, which offer a wider choice of goods. A number of these have been built in Ayr, such as Tesco in Racecourse Road, Safeway in Castlehill Road, and Asda, seen here in River Street. The shop was erected in 1986–7 to plans by Cowie, Torry & Partners and occupies the site of Newton Castle. (*Dane Love*)

# 2

# *Ayr at Work*

Stampworks, 1936. This group of workers was employed in the heat treatment department of the Scottish Stamping & Engineering Company's stampworks. The 'big' stampworks, properly known as the Neptune Works, was established in 1900 in West Sanquhar Road. (*Isobel McGarvey*)

Newarkhill Farm, *c.* 1935. Agriculture is one of the oldest industries in the district, and this postcard illustrates just one of many typical farms. Newarkhill Farm is located on the northern edge of the Carrick Hills, just above Alloway. When this photograph was taken Elizabeth Hutchison occupied the farm, which was part of the estate of Newark Castle, itself part of the Cassillis and Culzean estates, and for many years was tenanted, then owned, by the Hutchison family. A photograph of around 1860 exists showing the farm with a thatched roof. (*Author's Collection*)

Newarkhill Farm, 2003. As with many farms, Newarkhill is no longer in operation as an agricultural unit, the lands being sold off to leave only a 4-acre paddock attached to the house. It is now owned by the McNicols, who bought it in 1993. Newarkhill has one of the finest views over the town, being positioned 435 feet above sea level. (*Dane Love*)

Over Mills, *c.* 1950. There had been a mill on this site from at least the thirteenth century. It was initially used for grinding corn, but in 1761 a waulkmill was added for fulling, or beating, cloth, since when the name Over Mill became pluralised. The mill was powered by water diverted from the River Ayr, which was dammed by a major weir. It had a water wheel 20 feet in diameter, capable of producing thirty horsepower and driving five pairs of stones. Alterations to the mill, costing £531, were made in 1806. (*Author's Collection*)

Over Mills, 2003. The reliance on a steady source of water for power had long passed by the time the Over Mills were demolished in 1963. Latterly the mill was occupied by Thomas Steele, grain merchant. Only the lower walls and foundations of the mills survive, but the weir and the stepping-stones are still extant, the stones being a popular turning point for walkers following the riverside walk. (*Dane Love*)

Ayr Harbour, *c.* 1900. This early photograph depicts the north side of the harbour, with a cargo ship docked below the old steam crane. In the background can be seen the tall chimney of the saw mill in York Street, with lesser chimneys belonging to the Vulcan iron foundry beyond. The large shed to the right is unusual in that it has a large corner cut away, to allow trains to pass on the harbour branches. (*Ayrshire Archives – Valerie Dean*)

Ayr Harbour, 2003. The number of ships using Ayr as a port has declined in recent years, but a few still arrive and transfer cargoes on the north side of the harbour. This ship is the *Sea Eagle* of Bridgetown (formerly the *Shoreham* of Belfast). (*Dane Love*)

The harbour, *c.* 1905. This early view of the harbour was taken from the New Bridge looking seaward. The steel latticework bridge was erected in 1899 to allow the railway line from Ayr goods station to cross the water and reach the wharves on the south side of the river. A variety of ships can be seen in the basin, some of them sailing vessels, others powered by steam. The tall chimney in the distance belongs to the shipyard. (*Author's Collection*)

The harbour, 2003. Taken from the same corner of the New Bridge, the most obvious difference in the view is the loss of the railway bridge. The railway line was closed with the decline in shipping, leaving only sidings on the north side of the river. The bridge survived until 1978, when the steelwork was removed. The harbourside is now the home of a variety of upmarket flats, including Mariner's Wharf, Harbour Pointe and Churchill Tower. The pontoons are used for mooring yachts and other pleasure craft. (*Dane Love*)

Old Harbour, *c.* 1905. This view depicts South Harbour Street, with its warehouses on the left and the fish market in the centre. The turret of Miller's Folly can just be made out, and to its right the gable of Miss Janet Dunlop's inn. Behind this was the 21st Regimental Infantry barracks, headquarters of the Royal Scots Fusiliers. (*Author's Collection*)

Old Harbour, 2003. The wharves are still here, but the south side of the harbour has been virtually abandoned by boats and various blocks of flats now occupy the quays. The main blocks seen here are known as Harbour Pointe, dating from 2000. The old warehouses were destroyed by fire in about 1974 and the site of the barracks (closed in 1959) became Ayr swimming baths, erected in 1972 to plans by Cowie Torry & Partners. This was later extended to become the Citadel Leisure Centre. Only Miller's Folly remains unchanged. (*Dane Love*)

Fishing boat, 1991. Ayr Harbour has been a home to a fishing fleet for a number of centuries, but in the late 1990s the fishmarket was closed and the fleet relocated to Troon. Ayr was a port of registry, with the letters 'AR' used to indicate vessels registered there, although many 'BA', or Ballantrae, vessels used the port. (*Sheena Andrew*)

Fishing boat, 2003. With the removal of the fishing fleet, the south side of the harbour has been abandoned by the port authorities in favour of the northern side. Today South Harbour Street has been redeveloped with various blocks of flats erected along the quayside. This vessel, the *Kingfisher*, is used for pleasure fishing trips from Ayr. (*Dane Love*)

The harbour, *c.* 1912. Taken looking back towards the town (the Town Hall steeple is visible on the right), this view depicts the harbour at its busiest. Steamers and other vessels transported cargoes of all sorts from the port, including timber, coal and potash. The vessel on the left, with the twin funnels and winding gear, was the dredger, that to the right the *Ailsa*, of Leith. (*James McCarroll*)

*Inset:* The harbour, 2003. Only the north side of the harbour is now used for shipping, and this is on a smaller scale than previously. The pontoons here are used for pleasure craft, overlooked by the flats of Harbour Pointe. (*Dane Love*)

PS *Troon, c.* 1920. The *Troon* was built in 1902 for the Glasgow and South Western Railway Company by J.P. Rennaldson of South Shields. It was employed as a tug in Troon Harbour but was also used in Ayr, as seen in this view. On the left is the double-storey round Pilot House. The ship was sold to Middlesbrough Towage Company in 1930 before being broken up in 1948. (*Frank McKee*)

Ayr pilot boat, 2003. The harbour is still used for the importation of timber and fertilisers and the exportation of coal. Other goods are landed at Ayr, and at times the harbour pilot, the *Magnus*, seen here, is required to guide ships in and out of the Newton basin. There are two main goods terminals at Ayr, the Arran and Kintyre, both sporting large grey sheds. (*Dane Love*)

Ayr Shipyard, 1928. Shipbuilding has taken place at Ayr for centuries. Ayr Harbour Trustees constructed a new slip dock on the south side of the harbour in 1881. This was operated by Samuel MacKnight & Co. until 1902 when Ailsa Shipbuilding Co. took over. The yard built a variety of vessels, the largest being the *Lord Aberdeen* of 1,360 tons in 1889. This photograph was taken on 15 November 1928 and shows the launch of the third-last vessel to be built at Ayr, the *Ville de Papeete*. (*South Ayrshire Libraries*)

Mosshill industrial estate, *c.* 1990. The modern factories at Mosshill were erected from 1973, officially to employ redundant miners from the Doon Valley, but in fact they employed men from all over the district. At the time this photograph was taken the two factories were occupied by Digital Equipment, which made personal computers, and Prestwick Circuits, which manufactured printed circuit boards. At the time of writing the larger of the two factories is occupied by Jabil Circuit, which manufactures and assembles printed circuit boards. The Prestwick Circuits factory has closed, business being transferred to Irvine. (*Author's Collection*)

Templeton's woollen mill, *c.* 1965. Taken from Turner's Bridge across the River Ayr, this photograph shows part of the premises of James Templeton's woollen mill. The firm was founded in 1827 and produced carpets at their works in Fort Street, but this was destroyed by fire on 16 June 1876, killing twenty-nine. A new factory was built in Mill Street in 1878. The firm produced a variety of quality wools for knitting, including 'Ayrbeam', 'Ayrfleck', 'Mystic' and 'Sestal'. (*Fred Westcott*)

River Terrace, 2003. The former mill buildings were demolished and the present flats erected on the same site. Before Templeton occupied the old buildings they were home to Hyland's starch works, which closed prior to 1909. (*Dane Love*)

Tannery, 1987. In the nineteenth century Mill Street was home to a number of major industries in Ayr, including the power station, slaughter house and Ayr brewery. This photograph, taken before the buildings were demolished, shows what was Thomas Murray's ice factory (with the arched windows) next to Harry Beebee's tannery, which was previously owned by R. Dobbie & Company. The tannery, which has a louvred second floor to allow the drying of hides, was taken over by the Bridge of Weir Leather Company and closed in 1979. (*Fred Westcott*)

Mill Street, 2003. This part of Mill Street awaits redevelopment. From here to Kyle Street is a large area of ground which was previously occupied by Templeton's worsted spinning mills, the Kyle iron foundry and the Townhead works, all of which have long gone. There are proposals to erect a large retail centre here, but no work has started. (*Dane Love*)

Ayr County Hospital, *c.* 1900. Work on the construction of the hospital in Holmston Road was started in 1881, to replace the old Ayr fever hospital, which stood at the corner of Smith and Mill streets. The architect was John Murdoch. R.F.F. Campbell of Craigie opened the new hospital on 13 February 1883. At that time it had around seventy beds, forty of which were for medical and surgical cases, twenty for fever cases, and the rest for various convalescent and infant purposes. The hospital closed on 31 October 1991. (*South Ayrshire Libraries*)

Ayr Hospital, 2000. The present Ayr Hospital was erected on a greenfield site on the outskirts of the town and opened in 1991, designed by Keppie, Henderson of Glasgow. When it opened the former hospitals of Ayr County, Heathfield and Seafield were closed. A new day surgery unit and patients' hotel were added in 1993. The hospital copes with around 2,500 accident and emergency cases each month, as well as 10,000 appointments at the out-patients clinic. (*Medical Photography – Crosshouse Hospital*)

Ayr County Hospital, September 1985. Taken in one of the corridors of the former hospital, this photograph shows just how cramped and dated the hospital had become in its final years. (*Medical Photography – Crosshouse Hospital*)

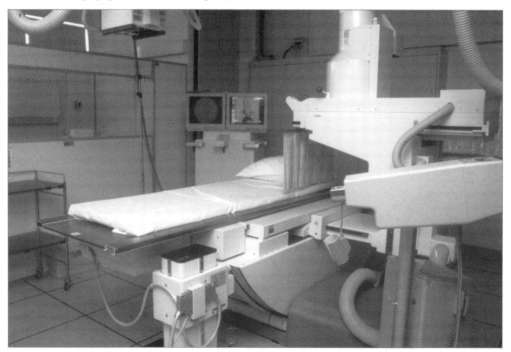

Ayr Hospital, *c.* 2000. Medical science has marched forward over the past hundred years or so. This photograph depicts the vascular angiograph suite in the new Ayr Hospital, shortly after its installation. (*Medical Photography – Crosshouse Hospital*)

John Sherry's market garden, c 1970. At the start of Holmston Road, on the north side, were the premises of John Sherry, who operated a small market garden from 1951 until 1973. There were at one time a few nurseries and gardens along Holmston Road and the previous occupant of this one was MacGill & Smith. In 1896 it was the Dennison Nursery. To the left of the bystanders are Station Road and the eastern station yard. The monumental sculptor next door was named Joseph Boyd – Joe Polson, who lived at Doonfoot, owned the business. (*John Sherry*)

Holmston Road, 2003. As part of road widening improvements the market garden was cleared away and a much wider Station Road was built, connecting with a roundabout at the junction with Holmston Road. This took place in 1977, when the Victoria Bridge was widened. Station Road and John Street thereafter became the main driving route around the centre of town, missing out the busy heart. When the greenhouse was demolished it was found to date from around 1890–8. (*Dane Love*)

Ayr tram, 1911. This photograph depicts tramcar no. 18 decorated for the coronation of King George V in 1911. It was built for exhibition purposes by Hurst Nelson of Motherwell in 1902. Here are the staff of the tram company, which was operated by the burgh council, dressed in their uniforms or best clothes for the occasion. The photograph was taken at Newton Park, the location of the workshops. The tram service in Ayr operated from 1901 until 1931, when it was replaced by buses. At its height in 1928, 5,743,663 fee-paying passengers were served. (*Author's Collection*)

Bus, High Street, 2003. After the trams were withdrawn at midnight on Hogmanay 1931 the service was replaced by buses, run by the Edinburgh-based Scottish Motor Traction company. Locally this firm was named Western SMT as of 1932. This firm was bought out by the large Stagecoach bus operating business in more recent years, and this Whitletts bus sports Stagecoach's blue, orange, red and white livery. (*Dane Love*)

Alloway railway station, *c.* 1920. The railway line through Alloway was created in 1906 as a link from Ayr through Dunure and Maidens to Turnberry. Known as the Dunure & Maidens Light Railway, the line was built for holidaymakers heading for Turnberry. The station was closed in 1930, but in 1947 it was reopened when the railway was reinstated as far as Butlin's holiday camp. The line was closed fully in 1968. (*James McCarroll*)

Alloway railway station, 2003. Since the railway line was lifted and the platform cleared away, the railway cutting has gradually reverted back to nature. Today the site of the station is little more than a hollow in the surrounding landscape, with trees growing alongside. On the opposite site of the hollow can be seen vehicles parked in Murdoch's Lone, the name of the roadway leading to the Tam o' Shanter visitor centre. (*Dane Love*)

Ayr station, *c.* 1985. Taken from the north side of the station, this view looks down over the platforms towards the main station buildings, with the prominent Station Hotel in the centre. The railway in the foreground was a branch that leads into a series of sidings, located alongside Smith Street. In the distance is the modern concrete office block of Burns House. (*Fred Westcott*)

Ayr station, 2003. The sidings alongside the main station have been lifted, and the site is now used for car parking. By the side of Smith Street are flats that were built as retirement homes. (*Dane Love*)

Ayr station, September 1985. This photograph shows the last steam locomotive, the *George Stephenson*, making its way from Ayr station. The interest in steam trains has attracted a large crowd, all keen to look back with nostalgia on the travel methods of yesteryear. (*Fred Westcott*)

Ayr station, 2003. After the last steam train had left Ayr the station was closed for refurbishment and the line was electrified. When it opened again in 1987 it was given the name Ayrline. The line remains popular today with commuters to and from Glasgow, as well as a stop on the route to Stranraer for Ireland. (*Dane Love*)

# 3

# *Health, Rest &*
# *Recreation*

Ayr beach, *c.* 1935. In the twentieth century Ayr awoke to its tourist-attracting qualities and began promoting itself as the ideal resort for 'health, rest and recreation.' On warm balmy summer days the beach was a magnet for locals and tourists alike, and could easily be as crowded as it was when this postcard was taken. (*Author's Collection*)

The Low Green and bandstand, *c.* 1900. One of Ayr's treasures, the Low Green was gifted to the burgh by royal charter in the fourteenth century. Since that time it has been used for a variety of pleasure purposes. This early postcard depicts the bandstand that stood on the green from around 1890 until 1951. It was a popular gathering place on summer evenings, when a variety of musicians were booked to entertain the crowds, made up of locals as well as holidaymakers. (*James McCarroll*)

Low Green, 2003. The bandstand has gone, leaving this part of the Low Green emptier. It is still used for a few travelling roadshows, however. In the distance the houses along the edge of the green remain relatively unchanged. The building on the right has been extended the most. Originally Glendoon House, it is now the Fairfield House Hotel. In the centre are the houses of Alloway Park, and to the left the house with the tower is located in Park Terrace. (*Dane Love*)

The Pavilion, *c.* 1914. The council erected the large theatre at the Low Green to plans of J.K. Hunter. Costing £8,000 and with seating for 1,500, it opened in May 1911 and was the location of many popular shows over the years. For about fifty years the famous theatrical Popplewell family ran the theatre, bringing well-known acts such as George Formby, the Merrymakers and Grace Clark and Colin Murray to Ayr. The fountain on the left is the Steven fountain, unveiled in September 1892. James Steven, a Glasgow ironfounder, gifted it to the town. (*Author's Collection*)

The Pavilion, 2003. Dubbed 'the white elephant by the sea' soon after it opened, the Pavilion has struggled to keep itself afloat over the years. As well as theatrical performances, it has been used for dances, discos and roller-skating, but in recent years the attraction became less popular. It has recently been restored and reopened as 'Pirate Pete's' children's indoor play area. (*Dane Love*)

Boating pond, *c.* 1930. The boating pond was located on the Esplanade, between Seabank Road and Cromwell Road. It was created in about 1925 with an adjoining playground complete with maze. (*Author's Collection*)

*Inset:* The Esplanade, 2003. The boating pond has long since been drained, the site now ready for redevelopment. The building with the tower is the Horizon Hotel, which claims to be Ayr's only seafront hotel. The hotel started off in a former house in Queen's Terrace, erected in 1845, but has been extended considerably seaward along Cromwell Road. (*Dane Love*)

The beach, *c.* 1950. As far as tourists and holidaymakers are concerned, the beach at Ayr is one of the highlights of the town. A wide stretch of golden sands, it extends 2 miles from the harbour mouth south towards Doonfoot. In warm summer months it can be packed with children enjoying the sands, building sandcastles and playing games. (*Author's Collection*)

The beach, 2003. The beach does not seem to have the same draw for modern children as it once had, but it can still be a popular attraction when the weather improves. Only on the warmest of bank holiday weekends does any semblance of the massive crowds swarming to the shore return. The Esplanade, however, remains popular with walkers, taking in the fresh air, as well as courting couples, 'cruisers' in their cars and dog walkers. (*Dane Love*)

Children's Corner, *c.* 1965. Occupying a corner of the Low Green, at the junction of the Esplanade with the continuation of Wellington Square, the children's play area was developed in the 1960s as an alternative to the beach, which could suffer from cool breezes. The intention was to extend the tourist season. As part of the plan new kiosks selling ice cream and hotdogs were introduced. (*Author's Collection*)

Children's adventure playground, 2003. The harsh and comparatively dangerous brick and concrete structures, as well as pools of water, were replaced with a new 'adventure' type playground in 1995, part of the funding coming from the European Union. Now climbing frames and sand pits are the thing, all having the benefit of bark on the ground to break any falls. (*Dane Love*)

Newton Shore, c. 1930. Newton-upon-Ayr has always been the poor neighbour on the north side of the river, and so it was with its beach. Stonier than the main Ayr beach and backed by the railway sidings and a fertiliser factory, nevertheless Newton Esplanade was a popular spot for locals. At one time it had a putting green. The wooden groynes were used to prevent coastal erosion. (*Author's Collection*)

Newton Shore, 2003. Even quieter than it once was, Newton Shore is today only frequented by walkers and the odd picnicker. It has more of a reputation as the spot where courting couples tend to go and spend time in their cars. The wooden groynes have succumbed to the elements, although fragments of them can still be seen. Instead, the less-attractive steel piles and mass concrete reinforcements have replaced them. (*Dane Love*)

*Manxman* at Ayr Harbour, *c.* 1969. Many vessels called at Ayr while taking trips 'doon the watter', or touring the west coast. The better known vessels were the *Juno*, which sailed from sail from Ayr until 1931, after which the *Duchess of Hamilton* replaced her. This photograph shows the *Manxman* at Ayr, ready for an Isle of Man trip. Note the old fishmarket on the other side of the harbour. (*Sheena Andrew*)

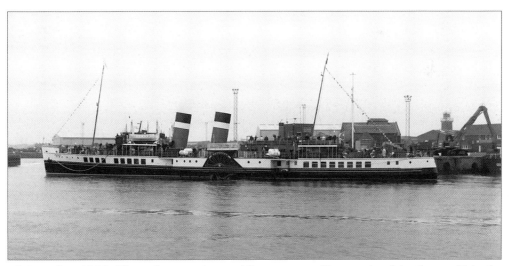

PS *Waverley*, 2003. The only sea-going paddle steamer still operational in the world is the well-known *Waverley*, seen here in Ayr in June 2003, its first visit after a multi-million pound refit. The vessel uses Ayr as a port on occasions, as part of its variable summer programme. On this occasion the boat left Ayr, called at Girvan, then circumnavigated Ailsa Craig before returning at eventide. (*Dane Love*)

The *Juno, c.* 1910. A number of pleasure steamers sailed from Ayr to ports such as Brodick on Arran, Campbeltown on Kintyre, or round the Kyles of Bute to Rothesay, Dunoon and other Clyde resorts. Seen leaving the harbour from the South Pier, the *Juno* was built for the Glasgow & South Western Railway Company. In 1923 she was repainted in London, Midland & Scottish railway colours, and continued to sail from Ayr until 1931, after which the *Duchess of Hamilton* replaced her. This vessel was built by Harland & Wolff at Govan and served until 1972. (*Author's Collection*)

The *Waverley*, 2003. Small passenger vessels that take tours around the islands in the Firth of Clyde still sometimes visit the harbour. One of these is the *Balmoral*, which is based in Bristol, but sometimes arrives in Ayr as part of sails organised by Waverley Excursions. The *Waverley* itself is better known, seen here arriving at Ayr. (*Dane Love*)

The Lunch Box snack bar, *c.* 1965. Built to the rear of 1 Queen's Terrace, and overlooking Bath Place towards the Low Green, The Lunch Box is only one of a number of cafés, snack bars and chip shops that have catered to the needs of the holidaymaker. (*Author's Collection*)

The Lunch Box, 2003. The café and carry-out snack bar is still serving the customers, offering a similar fare. Apart from the prices having increased, the café has increased in height, with the addition of a second storey above. (*Dane Love*)

The Sea Tower Hotel, *c.* 1960. There have been quite a few large houses in Ayr that have been converted into hotels or guesthouses, to cater for visitors to the town. The Sea Tower was originally erected as a private house in about 1860 for David Hunter but it was later converted into a luxury hotel. The sender of this postcard noted, 'this is just as nice as you said it would be. Quite a few honeymooners in just now.' The hotel boasted 'hot and cold, and gas fires in all bedrooms. Interior springs in all beds.' (*Author's Collection*)

The Sea Tower, 2003. The hotel was closed and the tower converted into private flats. To the rear of the building shown in the earlier view a wholly incongruous brick-built extension was added in 1977, one of the worst examples of poor planning in the town. (*Dane Love*)

Gartferry Hotel, *c.* 1969. Gartferry House was erected in Racecourse Road in 1867 to plans by Andrew MacLachlan. The house was built for Robert Paton, and incorporated into the surrounding wall are three stones that formerly supported the burgh gibbet on the Over Tolbooth. The house was converted into a hotel in 1930 by Fairbairns of Glasgow. (*Author's Collection*)

Gartferry Hotel, 2003. Still a popular establishment, the hotel has been extended to the rear, where the Commodore function room is popular for weddings. The hotel has sixteen en-suite bedrooms and an attractive Captain's Table restaurant. (*Dane Love*)

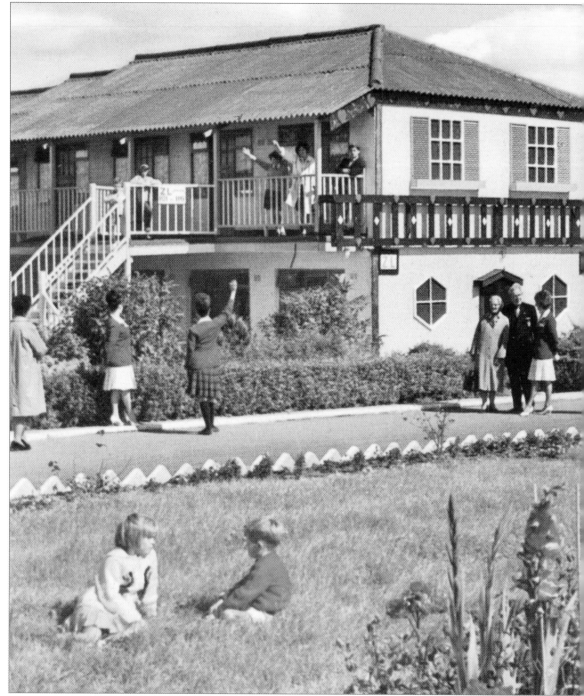

Cottage chalets, Butlin's holiday camp, *c.* 1960. The former HMS *Scotia* naval training camp was taken over by Billy Butlin, who converted it into a holiday camp. Thousands of holidaymakers came to Butlin's at Ayr for their summer break, staying in the painted chalets, unaware of their history. On offer were indoor and outdoor swimming, a theatre, cinema, church, fairground, miniature railway, dancing, ski-lift and a whole host of activities organised by the Redcoats. (*Author's Collection*)

Craig Tara holiday park, 2003. The demand for organised camp holidays fell dramatically in the 1970s with the advent of cheaper flights to warmer destinations in the Mediterranean and further afield. Despite reinventing itself as 'Wonderwest', the camp was closed and sold to Haven Holidays, who demolished most of the chalets and replaced them with static caravans, creating a new type of holiday park. Still on offer are indoor pools and shows, children's entertainment, bowling and amusements. As can be seen in this photograph, some of the original double-storey chalets survive, now named after golf courses. (*Dane Love*)

Cottage chalets, *c.* 1960. These old chalets were also part of the former naval training camp and after the Second World War were converted into holiday accommodation. Painted in bright colours and bordered by gardens, for many years they were holiday homes to thousands of families. (*Author's Collection*)

Caravans, Craig Tara, 2003. Today the site has over 800 caravans, of which 500 are privately owned, the remainder being offered for hire. There are also 116 holiday apartments (known as Burns Square) and 175 chalets within the complex. The caravans in this photograph overlook the pond, near to the shore. (*Dane Love*)

Skating rink, Butlins, *c.* 1960. Roller-skating was one of the main hobbies of the 1960s, and Butlin's holiday camp catered for those keen to take part. In the background is the prominent cliff known as the Heads of Ayr. (*Author's Collection*)

Go-kart track, Craig Tara, 2003. Roller-skating has come and gone, to be replaced by roller-blades. However, this picture shows the go-kart track at Craig Tara, almost on the same site as the picture above. (*Dane Love*)

St Andrew's House, *c.* 1950. St Andrew's was built in Seafield Road as a private house in the late 1800s in a style typical of the period. For a number of years it was owned by James W. Galloway and then his widow, Jessie. The Scottish Horse and Motormen's Association of Glasgow later acquired the house as a holiday and recuperation centre. Hundreds of sick workers came here for a rest away from their work. In later years the house was run by the association's successor, the Transport & General Workers' Union. (*Author's Collection*)

Creggan Bahn nursing home, 2003. St Andrew's House has been renamed and extended to form the Creggan Bahn nursing home. Here elderly residents can live in comfortable surroundings, receiving the care they need. The home, which is owned by Mrs M. Caldow, has thirty-two bedrooms and offers day care and respite nursing care for older people and those with a mental illness. (*Dane Love*)

# 4

# Honest Men
# & Bonie Lassies

Ayr Academy prize-winners, *c.* 1950. The rector at the time was Mr J. Douglas
Cairns. (*Author's Collection*)

Charles Galloway, *c.* 1950 Ayr has had a number of characters who were well known around the streets over the years. Among these were the 'Swan Lady', who fed the swans in the River Ayr on a regular basis. Another former character was Charles Galloway, who was noted for his skills on the fiddle. He often played at the Auld Brig o' Doon, attracting listeners from the many tourists who went there. As can be seen in this photograph, he was also well known to the local birdlife, which came down to eat from his hands. (*Author's Collection*)

Street entertainer, 2003. Buskers and entertainers can be found at a number of locations in the town centre. Some are musically talented, whereas others seem to have a cheek asking for money. This photograph is of a man who performs Andean pipe music, complete with microphone, speakers and amplifier, all powered by his portable generator. Not only does he collect money, he also sells copies of his CD entitled *Waykis*. The picture was taken next to the street sculpture known as 'The Poet and the World', which is next to Winton Buildings in the High Street. (*Dane Love*)

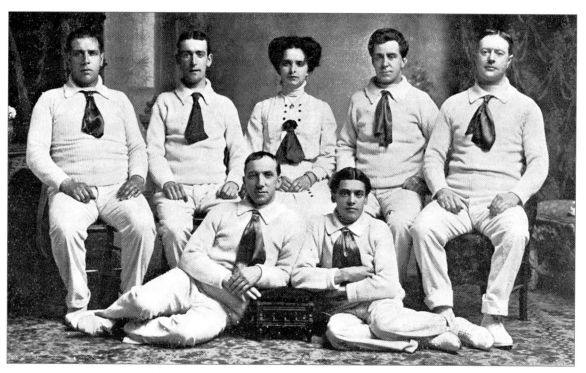

Ayr Entertainers, 1909. Jack Belton's Ayr Entertainers were one of a bunch of local performers who graced the stages of the local theatres, such as the Gaiety, Pavilion and Playhouse, which is now a bingo hall in Boswell Park. Other groups, which performed similar concerts, included Charlie Kemble's Super Entertainers and Lee & Arden's Entertainers. (*Author's Collection*)

Ayr Players, 1999. The Ayr Amateur Players were founded in 1925 but later shortened their name. They usually do two productions each year, in addition to a pantomime. This photograph shows a scene from *Honestly Now*, performed at the Civic Theatre. A breakaway group formed the Ayr Fort Players and another breakaway resulted in the Compass Club, both performing similar shows. The Ayr Players have their own clubroom in the former Cronies' Cabin in Craigie Road. (*Sandy Graham – Ayr Players*)

Ayr racecourse, *c.* 1915. The racecourse was laid out in 1907 over 1 mile 4 furlongs by the Western Meeting Club to replace the Old Racecourse on the south side of the town. The course is home to Ayr Gold Cup, which has been run since 1804, and which is now the richest race in Scotland. The Scottish Grand National has also been held at Ayr since 1966. This postcard depicts the Club Stand, erected in 1914 to replace the stand burned to the ground by suffragettes. (*James McCarroll*)

Ayr racecourse, 2003. Now the most important racecourse in Scotland, being the only grade one course in the country, Ayr attracts top horses and jockeys. Within the grounds can be seen a statue of the famous horse Red Rum, who won the Scottish and British Grand Nationals in 1974. The Western Meeting Club sold the racecourse in 2003 to the local consortium Pacific Shelf for £9.3 million. The original grandstand still exists in this photograph, and adjoining it to the left is the Princess Royal Stand, opened on 19 April 1996 by Princess Anne. (*Dane Love*)

Ayr tennis courts, c. 1926. Located on the grounds of the Citadel, the tennis courts were opened in August 1921 and Ayr Tennis Club was founded soon after. In the background is the tower of St John's, and to the right are the fine houses of Eglinton Terrace. This street was built in about 1855 and is named after the Montgomerie of Eglinton family who formerly owned the Fort. (*James McCarroll*)

Ayr tennis courts, 2003. The tennis courts and Eglinton Terrace remain virtually unchanged in what is a quiet corner of Ayr. Within Eglinton Terrace is the Bruce Hotel. (*Dane Love*)

Ayr Amateur Operatic Company, 1929. The Amateur Operatic Company in Ayr was founded in 1903 and their first major production, *HMS Pinafore*, was presented the following year. This photograph shows the cast of the 1929 production, *Floradora*, which was put on for six nights in February 1929 at Ayr's Playhouse, which was located in Boswell Park. The company had actually been in abeyance between 1914 and 1927, and this was their first production after that. (*Ayrshire Archives – Ayr Amateur Operatic Company*)

Ayr Amateur Operatic Company, 1992. The company celebrated their centenary in 2003. They are the only amateur operatic society in Scotland that puts on a show for two weeks in a professional theatre. A number of former members went on to act professionally, among them Walter Carr, noted for his part in *Para Handy*. This photograph shows the cast in the 1992 production of *My Fair Lady*. (*Ayrshire Archives – Ayr Amateur Operatic Company*)

Wellington School, *c.* 1970. The wife of an Ayr schoolmaster founded Wellington School in 1836. Originally located in Wellington Square – hence the name – the school moved to Carleton Turrets in 1923, from where it has expanded into various neighbouring properties. The school was originally a boarding school, the fees in 1926 being around 120 guineas per year. (*Wellington School*)

Wellington School, *c.* 2000. Today Wellington School is purely a day school, and it now caters for boys as well as girls, from age thirteen to eighteen. Approximately 550 pupils attend the school, studying to Advanced Higher level, and specialising in sport, music, drama and art. Among some well-known former pupils are broadcaster Kirsty Wark and model Kirsty Hume. (*Wellington School*)

Salvation Army, *c.* 1960. The Salvation Army in Ayr was established in 1884 and by 1905 was able to open its specially built citadel in New Road. This building was designed by Arthur Hamilton. In 1908 there was a major Christian revival organised in the town. At that time over one thousand men and women, often from irreligious backgrounds, were converted to Christianity. This photograph depicts the junior section of the Salvation Army band. (*South Ayrshire Libraries*)

Salvation Army, *c.* 1990. Seen marching along Main Street, the Salvation Army and its band are well known in the town for their good works. The citadel in New Road was closed in 2002, but there are plans for replacing it with an up-to-date citadel elsewhere, so that the work of the army can continue. (*Carl Huggins – Salvation Army*)

Buff Bill's parade, *c.* 1895. A number of travelling entertainers made a point of coming to Ayr on their circuit of the country. Buff Bill was a take-off of the Wild West show that toured with Buffalo Bill. Buff Bill came to Ayr sometime between 1893 and 1896. The real Buffalo Bill visited with his Wild West show on 12 September 1904 and performed two sell-out shows at Newton Park, comprising a cast of 800 and 500 horses. Three trains were required to transport the party. (*Ayrshire Archives – Valerie Dean*)

Holy Fair, 2003. A variety of major shows and exhibitions are held in Ayr throughout the year. These include the annual cattle show and flower show, both of which bring thousands of visitors to the town. The Holy Fair is a lower-key affair, held at Rozelle estate. Most of the exhibitors are local charities, who use the event as a major fund raising exercise. (*Dane Love*)

Ayr United, 1959. Ayr United was formed in 1910 when two local teams, Ayr FC (founded 1879) and Ayr Parkhouse FC (founded 1886) amalgamated, settling on Ayr's pitch at Somerset Park. Parkhouse previously played at Beresford Park. The team were to become Second Division champions in 1937, 1959, and 1988. This photograph shows a game taking place at Somerset Park against Montrose on 17 January 1959. (*Sheena Andrew*)

Ayr United, 2002. This more recent team photograph shows the squad that played in the CIS Insurance cup final against Rangers on 17 March 2002. This was the team's first appearance in a major cup final, but they were beaten by the Glasgow side 4 goals to nil. Just six days later Ayr played another significant match against Celtic in the Scottish Cup semi-final, again at Hampden Park, where they lost 3 goals to nil. Nevertheless, it was two significant high points for a club from the First Division. (*Mike Wilson – Ayrshire Post*)

Ayr Bowling Green, 1934. Ayr Bowling Club was founded on 17 March 1834 by thirty-six gentlemen in Ayr, most of whom were writers, officers, merchants or bankers. A green was laid off Wellington Square soon after, on what was the Washing Green, but it took until 1880 to pay off the club's early debts. A clubhouse was erected in 1859 and replaced with the present building in 1900. The photograph shows the Scottish Bowling Association President, David Kirkwood, throwing the silver jack at the club's centenary in 1934. Looking on is the club president, J. Melville Low. (*Ayr Bowling Club*)

Ayr Bowling Green, 1991. The lady president, in this case Mrs Betty Stewart, traditionally bowls the first bowl of the season. Looking on is club president Ian Low, grandson of the president in the older photograph. (*Ayr Bowling Club*)

Royal Scots Fusiliers, 1953. The Earl of Mar raised the regiment in 1678, and in 1707 this was renamed the North British Fusiliers, becoming Royal Scots Fusiliers in 1877. In 1908 the Territorial Army Act was passed, and the volunteer battalions became known as the 4th and 5th battalions, the 5th based at Ayr. In 1922 the two groups (the other from Kilmarnock) were merged to form the 4/5th Battalion. This photograph depicts the party that attended the coronation of Queen Elizabeth. (*B {RHF} Coy 52 Lowland Regiment*)

52 Lowland Regiment, Armistice, 2001. This photograph depicts the regiment grouped at the Royal Scots Fusiliers war memorial, which is located on the west side of the County Buildings. The memorial was erected in memory of those men who were killed in the Second World War, the statue sculpted by Pilkington Jackson in 1960. The Royal Scots Fusiliers served with the 52nd (Lowland) Division in the war, where one of its members, nineteen-year-old Dennis Donnini, was awarded the Victoria Cross posthumously. (*John Bradford – B {RHF} Coy 52 Lowland Regiment*)

Royal Scots Fusiliers, 1953. The Royal Scots Fusiliers, or Royal North British Fusiliers (Ayrshire's county regiment), existed until 1959 when it was merged with the Highland Light Infantry to form the Royal Highland Fusiliers. The Fusiliers are depicted taking part in a parade at Ayr's Churchill Barracks, which were located on the southern side of the harbour. It marked the presentation of new colours by G.H. Hughes-Onslow. The barracks were established in 1794, renamed after Winston Churchill in 1942 and were eventually closed in 1959. (B {RHF} Coy 52 Lowland Regiment)

B (RHF) Coy. 52 Lowland Regiment, Armistice, 2002. The Territorial Army still has two bases in Ayr. The B (RHF) Company of 52 Lowland Regiment has its headquarters at Seaforth Road, a combat (infantry) sub-unit, members of which are seen in the photograph. The other unit is A Squadron, The Queen's Own Yeomanry, which is a combat unit of the Royal Armoured Corps, based in Chalmers Road. (B {RHF} Coy 52 Lowland Regiment)

Guide Rally, 1957. The oldest guide company in Ayr was formed in 1911, shortly after the Guide movement was officially recognised by Lord Baden Powell. On 1 June 1957, to celebrate the centenary of Baden Powell's birth, the Ayrshire and Bute Girl Guide Association held a massive rally at Ayr racecourse, with thousands in attendance. This photograph was taken at that time, and shows a group of guides and their leaders demonstrating their skills in building a bonfire. (*Girlguiding Ayrshire South*)

Guides, *c.* 1970. Taken at Nether Auchendrane, where the local Guides have an activity centre, this photograph shows a group of girls in the early stages of building a camp fire. Today there are nine Guide companies in Ayr and Alloway, plus fourteen Brownie packs and eight Rainbow units for younger girls. (*Girlguiding Ayrshire South*)

# 5

# *There was a Lad*

Tam o' Shanter Inn, *c.* 1930. When this postcard was made Mrs Scott was the landlady of the famous inn associated with Robert Burns. The inn used the appeal of Burns to promote itself as the 'house where Tam o' Shanter and Souter Johnnie held their meetings', and over the doorway is a painting of Tam and Johnnie 'boozin' at the nappy'. Over the windows are cast-iron heads of Tam and Johnnie, popular on other inns at the time. Inside the inn visitors could see the stirrup cup and chairs. (*Author's Collection*)

Burns' Cottage, *c.* 1920. The 'auld clay biggin'' with its thatched roof is a mecca for lovers of the works of Robert Burns (1759–96), celebrated as Scotland's national bard. Burns' father, William Burnes (1721–84), erected the cottage, although the 'Janwar' win'' blew down a gable shortly after Burns' birth. Known as New Gardens at the time, William operated a market garden here. The Burns family moved from this cottage in 1766 to Mount Oliphant, still in Ayr parish, where William Burnes leased a few acres. This postcard depicts sheep being herded through the village, a most unlikely sight today! (*Author's Collection*)

Burns' Cottage, 2003. The simple thatched cottage is still preserved as a memorial to Burns, though at one time was used as an inn. Over the centuries a number of important visitors have made their way here, some like Wordsworth and Keats, being inspired to write poems of their own. Visitors visit the original byre first of all, where a film details the life of Burns, followed by the two main rooms of the cottage, where the bard was born. (*Dane Love*)

Burns' Cottage and Museum, *c.* 1930. After the Burns family left their cottage, it was purchased by the Incorporation of Shoemakers who converted it into a small alehouse. Early visitors were unimpressed by its use in this way, and in 1881 the Burns Monument Trustees acquired the cottage and restored it to its former appearance. In 1900 the adjoining museum was erected, to plans by Allan Stevenson, in which a number of early manuscripts and other relics were displayed. (*Author's Collection*)

Burns' Cottage and Museum, 2003. The museum has numerous priceless manuscripts and original artefacts associated with Robert Burns and his contemporaries. Here can be seen many of Burns' original letters and diaries, some of his and his friends' personal belongings, as well as paintings of the poet and others. There is also a gift shop. (*Dane Love*)

Alloway village, *c.* 1930. The vintage car and the tramlines date this view to the early 1930s. Alloway was a tiny village with little more than a single street of houses, a railway station and a smithy until the neighbouring town of Ayr began its outward spread. Opposite Burns' Cottage is a substantial terrace of double-storey houses, erected in 1903, and to this side of it is the village hall, erected in 1848 as the original school but rebuilt in 1929 as a public hall. Within are panels of plaster depicting scenes from Burns' poems. (*James McCarroll*)

Alloway village, 2003. Little has changed in the village street over the century, other than the tramlines have gone and cars are invariably parked in front of the houses and village post office. The surrounding countryside, however, has changed immensely, most of it having been built on to supply housing for an ever expanding town. (*Dane Love*)

lloway Auld Kirk, *c.* 1900. Celebrated in Burns' *Tam o' Shanter* as the place where the witches and arlocks enjoyed a dance, only to be disturbed by the shouts of Tam, the ruined church here dates from the xteenth century. Alloway was a separate parish from Ayr until 1691, when the two were joined. The nurch building was used as a school for a time, but the roof collapsed and it has stood in ruins ever since. uried in the kirkyard are Burns' father, William Burnes, Lord Alloway and Lt Gen. Hughes of Mount harles. (*Author's Collection*)

lloway Auld Kirk, 2003.
he old kirkyard attracts
any visitors for its Burns
nnections. The poet's
ther's grave is located at
e entrance, and a number
f his contemporaries are
so interred here, including
hn Tennant, the village
nith. In the kirk ruins can
e seen mortsafes, which
ate from the time of the
dy-snatchers. When this
otograph was taken the
nall belfry had been
moved because of its
nsafe condition. (*Dane Love*)

Burns Monument Hotel, *c.* 1910. The hotel here was first erected in 1829 and at that time was known as the Burns Arms Inn, operated by James Begbie. The hotel was built to cater for the growing number of tourists coming to see Burns' birthplace and associated landmarks, such as the Auld Brig o' Doon, located down the lane to the left. The hotel was later renamed the Burns Monument Hotel. The southern terminus of Ayr's tram system was outside the hotel, a tram being visible on the right. (*Author's Collection*)

Burns Monument Hotel, *c.* 1940. Noted for its 'Banks o' Doon tea gardens and luncheon rooms', the hotel supplied teas to visiting coach tours, including Ferguson's bus on the left. (*James McCarroll*)

Burns Monument Hotel, *c.* 1940. This aerial shot allows one to see the extent of the gardens both around the Burns Monument, as well as to the rear of the hotel. The Auld Brig o' Doon is seen above the monument, and in the foreground is the present Alloway parish church, erected in 1857–8, with its small cemetery behind.

Brig o' Doon Hotel, 2003. The Costley & Costley hotel group substantially rebuilt the hotel in the 1990s. Still as popular as ever, the hotel maintains its attractive gardens by the River Doon and is host to numerous weddings, one of which was in progress at the time the photograph was taken. (*Dane Love*)

Burns' Monument, *c.* 1950. The Grecian temple commemorating Robert Burns was erected between 1820 and 1823, the foundation stone being laid on 25 January (Burns' birthday) by Sir Alexander Boswell, son of the more famous James Boswell. The stone came from Cullala in Fife. Opened on 23 July (Burns' death date), the monument contains a small exhibition. The three-sided base represents the ancient divisions of Ayrshire – Carrick, Kyle and Cunninghame – and the nine pillars the muses. The monument, which rises 60 feet high, was designed by David Hamilton and cost £3,300 to build. (*Author's Collection*)

*Inset:* Burns' Monument, 2003. The monument and gardens are still popular with visitors, thousands flocking each year to visit it as part of Burns' Heritage Park. A carved stone from the first New Bridge (of Ayr) depicting the arms of the burgh, can be seen here. The former entrance gateway, seen here, is no longer the usual access to the gardens; access is now from a pathway starting at the Tam o' Shanter Experience visitor centre. (*Dane Love*)

Burns' Monument, *c.* 1920. Taken from within the gardens, this early postcard depicts the memorial and one of the gardeners who were employed to maintain the site to the highest standard. A second building within the gardens houses statues by James Thom of Tam o' Shanter and Souter Johnie. (*Author's Collection*)

Burns' Monument, 2003. The bushes and trees in the gardens are all much taller and fuller, obscuring the clear views of the monument seen in the early postcard. Within can be seen a display on Burns' life, and a small set of steps leads to the floor of the open colonnade, from where a view of the gardens and adjoining area can be enjoyed. (*Dane Love*)

Banks o' Doon tea gardens, *c.* 1940. The tea gardens adjoining the Burns Monument Hotel were laid out soon after the hotel was erected. According to the *New Statistical Account* of 1837 the hotel offered 'excellent fare at moderate expense, and kind and civil treatment'. On the opposite side of the lane from the tea gardens are the Burns Monument Gardens, also attractive. This postcard shows the gardens as viewed from the Auld Brig, looking towards the New Bridge, which had been erected across the River Doon in 1816. (*Author's Collection*)

Brig o' Doon tea gardens, 2003. The gardens are maintained largely for their attractiveness in wedding photographs. Hardly a week goes by without a number of brides and grooms being photographed in the gardens, with the arch of the Auld Brig o' Doon behind. (*Dane Love*)

Auld Brig o' Doon, *c.* 1940. The high-arched bridge was erected in the fifteenth century and was the main route across the Doon to the south of Ayr. Today it is bypassed by the New Bridge. The bridge was made famous in Burns' *Tam o' Shanter* as the spot where the witches chasing Tam are turned back, unable to cross running water. However, they manage to grab a hold of the tail of Tam's 'grey mare, Meg', and yank it from its rump. There are supposed to be cobbles with the footprints of the horse in them on the bridge, but the tale was pure fabrication! (*Author's Collection*)

Auld Brig o' Doon, 2003. The bridge was in danger of being demolished once the New Bridge was erected, but a group of Burns enthusiasts organised by Revd Hamilton Paul ensured its survival. (*Dane Love*)

Tam o' Shanter Inn, *c.* 1930. The High Street public house is celebrated as the place where Tam o' Shanter and his drouthy cronies met prior to Tam's famous ride from the witches. The truth is different, however, for Tam was, of course, a figment of Burns' imagination, and when the poem was written this building was just a house. It was later converted to an inn, and an enterprising landlord adopted the present name. (*Author's Collection*)

Tam o' Shanter Inn, 2003. The inn was purchased by the Town Council in 1944 for £4,000 and converted into a museum in 1957. The museum ran into financial difficulties and in the early 1990s was sold and converted back into a public house, which opened in 1993. The inn remains one of very few thatched buildings in Ayrshire today and is a fine example of eighteenth-century architecture. Over the pend a few lines from Burns' poems are still highlighted. (*Dane Love*)

Burns' statue, *c.* 1920. The statue of our national bard was unveiled on 8 July 1891 before an audience of 4,000 onlookers. The sculptor was George Lawson and the base, which depicts scenes from Burns' life and works, was the work of James Morris. The ornate wrought-iron railings were a victim of Second World War iron collections. (*Author's Collection*)

Burns' statue, 2003. The statue still stands in the midst of what was named Burns Statue Square, although the introduction of trees and bushes has tended to obstruct distant views of it. (*Dane Love*)

Auld Brig, *c.* 1920. The bridge across the River Ayr has stood since the fifteenth century. The burgh charters refer to it in 1440 and in 1491 King James IV crossed it, giving 10 shillings to the masons working on it. The bridge is celebrated in Burns' poem 'The Twa Brigs', in which the Auld and New bridges argue over each other's merits, and in which the Auld Brig predicts that the New Bridge would collapse. The New Bridge of 1786–8 did, in fact, succumb in a flood and was replaced by the present bridge of 1877–9. (*James McCarroll*)

Auld Brig, 2003. Bypassed by the later bridge, the Auld Brig survives as a popular footpath over the river. The bridge was in danger of demolition because of its poor condition at the end of the nineteenth century, and Sir William Arrol, who lived in Ayr (and is noted as the designer of the Forth Bridge), proposed erecting a replica in its place. An appeal by Burns enthusiasts raised £10,000, which enabled the bridge to be restored, between 1907 and 1910. On the bridge is an old sundial, and plaques commemorating Burns and the bridge's restoration. (*Dane Love*)

Auld Brig, *c.* 1940. This view was taken looking west, with the New Bridge visible through the arches of the Auld Brig. Some of the buildings backing on to the river – including a pawnbrokers, Findlay's, and Jacksons, the latter selling boots, shoes and raincoats – have painted advertisements. (*Frank McKee*)

Auld Brig, 2003. Most of the older High Street buildings have been demolished and replaced by later buildings, notably Marks & Spencer on the left. (*Dane Love*)

# 6

# *Around & About*

Sea front, *c.* 1950. This aerial view picks out some of the main locations on the shore side of the town. In the top left is Wellington Square, overlooked by the Sheriff Court and county buildings. The street on the bottom left is Queen's Terrace, probably erected in about 1845. The Pavilion Theatre is the building with the four towers on the edge of the Low Green, and on the top right is Fairfield House Hotel, formerly Glendoon House. (*Author's Collection*)

Greenan Castle, *c. 1930*. Perched precariously on its cliff top beyond Doonfoot, Greenan Castle was erected in about 1603 by John Kennedy of Baltersan. It probably occupies the site of an earlier fortified building, and even earlier earthworks surround the headland. It was from Greenan that Sir Thomas Kennedy, son of the 3rd Earl of Cassillis, left one morning in 1602 only to be murdered by Thomas Kennedy of Drummurchie in a family feud on the sands of Ayr shore. (*Author's Collection*)

Greenan Castle, 2003. The castle still stands on its headland, but this is gradually being eroded by the timeless action of the waves. Strengthened by various renovations during its life, there is little more that can be done to prevent it collapsing into the sea some day. (*Dane Love*)

Doonfoot, *c. 1935*. A small community has existed at Doonfoot for many years. The Doon was bridged here in 1772, Robert Burns' father-in-law being one of the masons employed on it, and a variety of cottages and businesses sprung up. This was also the site of Doonfoot Mill, latterly the Greenan Laundry. The present bridge dates from 1861. The building shown is Doonfoot Stores, at the time of the postcard occupied by James McCutcheon, who ran a market garden here as well as the grocery. The building was at one time known as the Low Bridge of Doon. (*Liz Kelly*)

Doonfoot, 2003. Only in recent years has the Doonfoot Stores been converted into the Secret Garden Restaurant. The view remains much as it was, though. (*Dane Love*)

Doonfoot Garage, *c.* 1935. This postcard shows the view across the traffic island in the opposite direction from the previous old photograph. The garage at Doonfoot was created out of an older building. At the time this photograph was taken it was run by Robert M. Smith who, as can be seen, operated a taxi service as well as selling BP fuel. (*Liz Kelly*)

Doonfoot Garage, 2003. The old garage building has long gone, and has been replaced by a modern car showroom. This was formerly an agent for Honda cars, but at the time of writing the County Saab dealership occupied it. The traffic island at the end of Greenfield Avenue has mostly been removed, leaving just small islands with illuminated bollards. Only the wall on the edge of the Belleisle estate and the cottages in Doonfoot Road remain much the same. (*Dane Love*)

Longhill Avenue, *c.* 1915. The roadway linking Alloway with Doonfoot on the south side of the River Doon is known as Longhill Avenue. At the beginning of the twentieth century it was a rural lane, renowned for its avenue of trees. Locally it was also known as 'Kate's Avenue', the Kate supposedly being the last leper who lived in a colony that may have existed hereabouts. The cottage in the postcard is known as The Glen, a little stream dropping from Newark Hill being located behind it. (*Author's Collection*)

Longhill Avenue, 2003. The main trees in the avenue were felled in 1962 and the whole area is now a desirable suburb of Ayr. The Glen cottage still survives, but numerous large bungalows and houses surround it. The scheme of bungalows incorporating Portmark Avenue on the north of the Avenue was erected in 1973. (*Dane Love*)

Belleisle House, *c.* 1935. Belleisle estate was originally part of the burgh lands of Ayr, but these were broken up and sold off in lots. This part was purchased by Hugh Hamilton who named his new home after a plantation he owned in Jamaica. Belleisle House was erected in two phases, the first in 1787 and the second in 1829. The house passed through various families until it was acquired by Ayr burgh on 15 May 1926 for £25,000. (*Author's Collection*)

Belleisle House Hotel, 2003. The house remains unchanged on this front, having been converted into a hotel shortly after being acquired by the council. To the rear and north side, however, extensions have been added to create a clubhouse for the Belleisle and Seafield golf courses, as well as a large function suite. The hotel has fourteen bedrooms and offers meals and snacks to non-residents. (*Dane Love*)

Belleisle estate, *c.* 1960. Apart from two golf courses, the grounds of Belleisle contain an attractive park with extensive walled gardens, conservatory, aviary and pet corner, deer park and other attractions. This view of the pond overlooks the flower beds in the walled garden towards the conservatory, in which are various exotic plants. The obelisk on the left contains inscriptions detailing verses from the Bible suitable for prayer. (*Author's Collection*)

Belleisle estate, 2003. The gardens are still a popular attraction, remaining relatively unchanged over the years. Also in the grounds of the estate are two golf courses, the Belleisle and Seafield courses, both eighteen holes in length. (*Dane Love*)

Eglinton Terrace, *c.* 1910. Eglinton Terrace, seen to the left of the Fort Castle, dates from around 1855. It was named after the Earl of Eglinton who formerly owned these lands. The family surname is Montgomerie, used for the name of another terrace on the opposite side of the open ground surrounding the tower. (*James McCarroll*)

Eglinton Terrace, 2003. Today Eglinton Terrace remains a salubrious line of houses, little changed from when they were built. Trees now obliterate views of St John's Tower, and the ubiquitous motor vehicle occupies most of the roadsides. (*Dane Love*)

Fort Castle, *c.* 1910. John Miller constructed this mock castle in 1853 as a house, incorporating the ancient tower of St John's Church. The church tower dates from the fifteenth century, but was taken over by Oliver Cromwell's soldiers and converted into a lookout for the new fort he erected in 1652. Miller (1820–1910), who made his fortune in India, purchased the barony of Montgomeriestoun and began developing it. 'Baron' Miller was also responsible for the little turret, which still stands overlooking the harbour and is affectionately known as 'Miller's Folly'. (*Author's Collection*)

St John's Tower, 2003. After Miller's death, Fort Castle was offered for sale at £2,700. In 1914 the 4th Marquess of Bute, who was a keen historian, acquired it. He demolished Miller's additions and rebuilt the tower in its original style. In 1986 the immediate surroundings were excavated, revealing the bases of pillars and other foundations. The tower is open to the public on 'Doors Open Day'. (*Dane Love*)

Fusilier's statue, *c.* 1905. Standing in Burns Statue Square is the war memorial of the Royal Scots Fusiliers, commemorating those who died in the campaigns in South Africa, Sudan and Burma. The people of Ayrshire, Wigtownshire, Kirkcudbrightshire and Dumfriesshire, the recruiting area of the Fusiliers, raised funds for its erection. The statue was sculpted by Thomas Brock and the memorial was unveiled in November 1902. The row of houses in the background is known as Killoch Place, with the studio of Wilhelm Hess, a noted photographer in Ayr at the time. (*Author's Collection*)

Fusilier's statue, 2003. The statue has been moved a few times as a result of various schemes that changed the road layout in the Square. The Royal Scots Fusiliers were founded in 1678 and existed until 1959 when they were merged with the Highland Light Infantry, creating the Royal Highland Fusiliers. (*Dane Love*)

Dalblair Road, *c.* 1995. Taken shortly before they were to be demolished, this photograph depicts what was latterly Ayr indoor market. Previously there were rather large semi-detached houses in this part of the street, that to the right being remains of two, but over the years most of these were rebuilt or replaced with other commercial properties. (*Fred Westcott*)

Dalblair medical centre, 2003. A modern block of offices and retail units, incorporating a medical centre, were erected on the site of the indoor market in about 2000. Only the lamppost remains unchanged in the two pictures. (*Dane Love*)

Ayr County Hospital, 1998. With the opening of the new Ayr hospital in 1991 the former Ayr County Hospital was closed. The building remained standing for a number of years before it was demolished to allow the site to be redeveloped. (*Fred Westcott*)

Holmston Road, 2003. These new blocks of flats, known as Riverside Walk, were erected on the site of Ayr County Hospital. On the opposite side of the street, on what was at one time Appleyard's Garage, more flats are being erected in 2003, named Holmston Gardens. (*Dane Love*)

King Street car park, *c.* 1980. Taken from the upper floors of the police station, this view looks over the ground between Wallace and Garden streets, south of King Street. The building on the left is the former Evangelical Union Church, erected in 1799 as a Burgher church. To its right is the back of the Black Bull Inn and other premises in River Street. Beyond can be seen the large bulks of British Home Stores (1984), Marks & Spencer (1974) and the telecommunications offices in the distance, dwarfing the tower of Holy Trinity Church. (*Fred Westcott*)

Asda, 2003. A few other buildings were demolished (including the church) before the Asda supermarket was erected on the site. It, and its car park, are seen here from the police station, and occupy land where at one time Newton Castle stood. This was an ancient castle owned by the Wallace family. At a later date there were aerated water works, a smithy and other commercial premises here. (*Dane Love*)

Belmont signal box, 1985. The signal box at Belmont was a prominent landmark in the Maybole Road area. It stood on the south-east side of the level crossing. (*Fred Westcott*)

Belmont level crossing, 2003. The signal box was demolished shortly after the upper photograph was taken, and no trace of it remains, the ground on which it stood now being incorporated in the adjoining garage. The level crossing on Belmont Road is automatically controlled. The houses in the background belong to Fenwickland Avenue, erected in 1955. (*Dane Love*)

Holmston Farm, 1987. Holmston Farm stood by the side of the Cumnock road, on the east side of Ayr, next to the junction with Overmills Road. The farm was at one time part of Holmston estate, but this was broken up and it became part of Auchincruive estate in 1781. (*Fred Westcott*)

Whiteford View, 2003. The lands of Holmston Farm were developed for housing in recent years, and Whiteford View stands on ground that was at one time the farmyard. The houses were erected in 1988 as part of the Hazelbank development by John Lynch Homes. (*Dane Love*)

River Ayr walk, *c.* 1915. This postcard depicts the riverside walk near to the old limekiln. A hundred yards downstream is Wallace's Heel. Here the freedom fighter, Sir William Wallace, managed to escape pursuing Englishmen by jumping from the side of the river. His foot is supposed to have left a mark on the rock, which is still visible. There is also a natural spring at this point and for many years there was an iron cup with which to drink. (*Author's Collection*)

River Ayr walk, 2003. The footpath alongside the River Ayr was created in 1910 when J.A. Campbell, owner of Craigie estate, decided to allow the public access to his grounds. The walk starts in Holmston Road and makes its way alongside the southern side of the river as far as the stepping stones at Over Mills. It then returns along the north side of the river, a circuit of almost 4 miles. Still popular with dog walkers, it has been converted into a cycle route as far as Auchincruive. (*Dane Love*)

Stepping stones, *c.* 1920. There has been a ford and stepping stones across the River Ayr at this point for many years. At one time there was a roadway from Whitletts down past Mainholm Tileworks (where there was a curling pond) to the ford, and thence south past the Over Mills to Holmston. The route of this road is still visible in places, but today only walkers frequent it. This postcard view of the stepping stones is taken looking north. The stones were reset in 1938. (*Author's Collection*)

Stepping stones, 2003. The stepping stones, which today are actually large cast concrete blocks, still allow walkers to cross the river. The ford has long gone, there being no need for vehicles to cross the river at this point. In any case, just downstream from the ford is the Overmills Bridge on Ayr bypass, erected in 1963. (*Dane Love*)

Auchincruive estate, *c. 1935*. Auchincruive estate is ancient, having been owned by the Wallaces at the time of Sir William Wallace, who is known to have hid hereabouts. The present house (known as Oswald Hall after later owners) was erected in 1767 by Robert Adam. In 1927 the estate was gifted to the West of Scotland Agricultural College as a new campus, the college moving here from Kilmarnock. The building in the distance in this postcard is Gibbsyard, the main stable block of the former estate. In the foreground is the Poultry School. (*Author's Collection*)

Auchincruive estate, 2003. Now part of the national Scottish Agricultural College, Auchincruive is just one of their three campuses. Here students are taught various courses, mainly to do with agriculture, poultry, horticulture, landscape management and other country-based professions. The photograph is taken from Oswald's Temple, a teahouse built on the summit of a low hill in 1778 to plans of Robert Adam. At the time of writing in 2003 there are proposals to close the college, but campaigns are under way to try to save it. (*Dane Love*)

# ACKNOWLEDGEMENTS

The author would like to extend his thanks to the following individuals and organisations for their assistance during the production of this book, be it supplying photographs, information, or in some other way:

In alphabetical order, they are: Grant Allan, Sheena Andrew (for her own photograph, as well as those of her late husband, Ken Andrew), Chic Carleton, Jim Eckford (Ayr Bowling Club), Sandy Graham, Carl Huggins (Salvation Army), Elizabeth Kelly, Sandra McCallum (Girlguiding Ayrshire South), James McCarroll, Karen McDermid (Craig Tara Holiday Park), Isobel McGarvey, Frank McKee, Philip Mancini, Steve Palmer (Ayrshire & Arran Health Board), Gordon Picken, Moira Rothnie, John Sherry, Captain Taplin (B(RHF) Coy 52 Lowland Regiment), Alistair M. Tyre (Ayr Amateur Opera Company), Ann Watson, Wellington School, Sheila West and other staff at the Carnegie Library in Ayr, Fred Westcott, Kevin Wilbraham (Ayrshire Archives), Andrew Wilson and Mike Wilson (*Ayrshire Post*).